THE SECRETS OF BUILDING A WEBSITE THAT WILL GROW YOUR BUSINESS

What you really need in a website to be found on Google

Angela Fairbanks

Wilbanks Publishing

ISBN-9798620531707
ISBN-10: 1477123456

Library of Congress Control Number: 2018675309
Printed in the United States of America

DEDICATION

This book is dedicated to my Lord and Savior Jesus Christ.
"With Christ, all things are possible," Phil 4:13

With special thanks to my Father, Harry, for instilling in me his entrepreneurial spirit. To my husband Tim, for his never-ending love and support. And mostly to my son and business partner Tyler, because without him, none of this could be possible.

THE SECRETS OF BUILDING A WEBSITE THAT WILL GROW YOUR BUSINESS

What you really need in a website to be found on Google

by
Angela Fairbanks

Foreword

This is a simple guide for the do-it-yourself (DIY), beginning website builder who wants to achieve a business website that will actually deliver results.

It will not teach you the steps of actually composing your website, but rather the components you will want to build into your website in order to show up in a Google search.

It is step-by-step, easy-to-follow and written in terms that are easy to understand. It is not meant to be a comprehensive guide for the experienced web designer, but is meant rather for someone who is just starting out with on a DIY web-designing platform such as Weebly, Wix, Squarespace, Wordpress, etc. That's not to say experienced designers won't learn something, but my intention is to help newcomers build a strong, solid site that will help them rank well in a Google search.

It is also for small business owners who want to see improvements with their online visibility, but don't really have the budget to hire a fancy, expensive firm. These are practical and effective steps that I have presented in a clear and easy-to-follow manner that most people should be able to follow with basic computer knowledge.

I have been a marketer since 2010, and though I don't control Google, I do know what they are looking for in a website. If you follow the steps I have outlined in this book, you will be well on your way to getting to that coveted first page ranking. I certainly can't promise you results, but I can tell you that every client for whom we've followed these techniques, are on the first page.

Many of these techniques may be new to you. All of them are above-board and real. We do not use any black-hat types of tricks or tips. If you are looking for a quick, sly or sneaky way to zoom to the top of page one using underhanded methods, this is not the book for you. All the methods in this book are ethical, tested and proven effective.

What Google wants today are websites that are

easy to maneuver and helpful to the user, with lots of great content. You will want to take into account their quality guidelines. They want a website to be informative, accurate, relevant, and mobile-responsive. Getting your website to rank well won't happen overnight, but with persistent and consistent attention, it will happen.

I've included a bonus section towards the end which will give you some advanced SEO techniques to launch you further ahead. While these are not necessary to get you to appear in a Google search, these tasks will go a long way to advance your website in rankings. Implement these bonus steps as you can.

Enjoy!

THE SECRETS OF BUILDING A WEBSITE THAT WILL GROW YOUR BUSINESS

What you really need in a website to be found on Google

Foreword

1. What Your Website is Actually Supposed to Do

2. Update Your Website Weekly, or at Minimum, Monthly

3. Your Website Should Link to Other Useful Information Sources

4. Your Website Needs at Least Three Points of Contact

5. Does Your Website Have Target Keywords?

6. Does Your Website Have Links to Your Social Net-

working Sites?

7. Does Your Website Have the Ability to Capture Leads?

8. Does Your Website Have an Active Blog?

9. Does Your Website Have Videos on it?

10. Is Your Website Mobile-Responsive?

11. Is There a Testimonial on the Home Page?

12. Is a Custom Domain With a Keyword Attached to Your Website?

13. Is There Unique Content on Every Page?

14. Is There a Custom Title Tag (H1 or H2) on Every Page?

15. Do the Website Pages Have Title Tags?

16. Is There an Internal Link Strategy in Place?

17. Do All Images Contain Alt Tags and Keywords?

18. Does Each Image Have a Proper Url and Filename?

19. Are There Meta Descriptions on Every Page?

20. Has the Google Business Page Been Verified and Optimized?

21. Is There an SSL Certificate Attached to the Site?

22. Are Google Webmaster Tools Being Utilized?

23. Has a Sitemap Been Submitted to Google?

24. Are There Social Media Connections in Place?

25. Has Duplicate Content Been Eliminated?

26. Have All Dead Pages Been Cleaned Up?

27. Has the Site Been Submitted to the Top 50 Online Directories?

28. Have Google Analytics Been Installed and Utilized?

Bonus Section

29. Is Email Marketing in Place That Drives Traffic Back to the Site?

30. Is There a Special Report or Checklist to Give Away?

31. Are Relationship Nurturing Autoresponders Enabled?

32. Are Reviews Being Posted to Google Business Page?

33. Are There Relevant Articles Showcasing Your Expertise?

34. Is There an Active Pay Per Click Campaign?

35. Is the Blog Connected to Social Bookmarking Sites?

36. Are There Social Sharing Capabilities on All Articles, Blogs, Content?

37. Is There a LinkedIn Company Page?

38. Is There an RSS Feed?

39. Is There a Reputation Marketing Strategy in Place?

40. Is There a Link to a Podcast on the Website?

41. Is there personal branding of the business owner?

42. Are there new and relevant plugins?

43. Are comments enabled to encourage engagement?

44. Are press releases done quarterly?

45. Is a newsletter or mini-course offered to establish authority?

1. WHAT YOUR WEBSITE IS ACTUALLY SUPPOSED TO DO

A website is the foundation for building a local web presence. If you do not have a website, then we encourage you to get one, or to build one yourself, right away. I'm going to assume you either have one or are preparing to build one.

Your website needs to serve a specific goal, and for most individuals and companies, the goal is to capture leads and effectively communicate with potential clients and customers.

If you have not been on your site for quite some time, please take the time and look at each component of your website. Is your Website current and up-to-date? Is all the information accurate?

What additional information can you share

with the public that would enhance their user experience when visiting you site? Does your site load quickly? People won't wait around for a slow, bogged-down site.

Make sure your site is not stuffed with a bunch of irrelevant ads. That's annoying. Google is all about 'user experience' right now, so try to keep that in mind as you are going through each step. With each step, ask yourself, "What can I do with this step to enhance the user experience?"

You want to communicate the main aspects of your business to the public via your website. That is going to mean your services, your location, your story, possibly the history of the company (which could be part of the story), your staff, your contact information, a pictorial gallery, etc. Sometimes the information you need to convey can literally be covered in one page—a simple landing page. But sometimes, you need to go much more in-depth and you need a multi-page, organized website in order to communicate properly what it is you do.

You also want to convey to the world that *you* are the expert in your field. YOU are the one who deserves the call. *You* are the one who is going to save the day for Mr., Mrs. or Ms. Customer who has the problem that *you* are going to be able to solve.

It goes without saying that your website should be free of spelling and punctuation errors. Have many people look over your site. If possible, have a professional editor look it over. Try to make it as perfect as you possibly can.

Lastly, make sure your website is attractive. Use eye-pleasing color combinations and stay away from hard-to-read combos like white text on a red background, unless it is absolutely necessary, or in small punches.

Your website needs to cover *all* of that. Does it?

2. UPDATE YOUR WEBSITE WEEKLY, OR AT MINIMUM, MONTHLY

Every good relationship begins with having strong communication. Your current and potential customers need to able to connect with you. One easy way to begin building trust and engaging them is to provide relevant and current information. The more fresh content you supply on a consistent basis, the more visitors you will have to your site. As you update your site, you will also help improve your Google rank. I recommend you update your site at least once per week.

If you will make out a simple calendar for the month and put things on there that will be of benefit to your readers, that's half the battle. For instance, every Friday, post about something. Down below I list some very simple ideas to get you started.

Here is an easy way to go about doing this. Sit down with a calendar from the dollar store. On your posting days, let's say Fridays, let's use the schedule below. Fill in specifics about which items you are going to post on your blog or gallery page of your website. This could be an item you pull from your Facebook page or other Social Media channel; it doesn't necessarily need to be new content every single time. Jot that down in the calendar space.

Next, sit down at your computer and go into the blog section and begin entering your information, scheduling your blogs/videos/posts for the dates listed on your calendar. That's it! Super easy. To go a step further, take that same content and schedule that on your social media channel. You can do this directly from the Facebook scheduler, or you can utilize a third-party scheduling program like Hoot Suite. There are several good ones out there.

There are literally hundreds of ideas out there of things you can post on your website. The bottom line is to make it relevant, make it about your business and make it helpful for your reader. You want Google to look at your content and announce "Hey, this guy has some great stuff going on over here! Let's send some traffic over his way!"

- 1st Friday: a video about your business
- 2nd Friday: an article you have written
- 3rd Friday: pictures of an event you've held, someone you've helped, inspirational, etc.
- 4th Friday: do a blog post asking your readers what they need help with, or answer an FAQ

If you simply cannot update your website weekly, opt for a more comprehensive update monthly. Treat it more like a "Here's what's been going on with us this month" type of air and give your readers a strong update of what has been happening in your business, remembering to work in several of your keywords in your copy. We'll cover keywords, what they are exactly and what importance they play, in an upcoming chapter.

Note, your updates don't need to all be a blog post. They can be photo and/or video additions, copy additions or rewrites, etc.

3. YOUR WEBSITE SHOULD LINK TO OTHER USEFUL INFORMATION SOURCES

Helping both customers and potential customers solve simple problems builds trust and credibility. People are more likely to buy from people whom they trust and have built credibility with. Google also looks favorably on sites that not only have *quality* incoming links, but also link to other *relevant* information. Please note, the information that you choose to link to needs to be *accurate and timely*. These links add to your website and do not take away from it. So, identify websites that your clients will find useful and set up the links today!

As a general rule of thumb I stick with:

- Authority sites*—those very popular with a huge crowd following like Amazon, YouTube, Pinterest, Ebay, etc. These are just a few.

- .gov sites

- .org sites

- .edu sites

    *Do not under any circumstances link to any illegal sites or sites with questionable ethics. If you have to ask whether or not what they are doing is legal, I'd advise you to stay away. There are many popular, above-board authority sites to link to!

    Let's walk through a practical example of this, always keeping in the front of our minds that Google wants our websites to be helpful, informative, and relevant. I am going to give you some examples of how a plumber could link to some solid, external sites that could/would be of potential value to the reader.

    Example 1: He could have a blog post that demonstrates how to winterize outside water spigots the late fall. In that blogpost, he could have a link to his YouTube channel. He is taking people offsite, but to his YT video.

    Example 2: Maybe in another article, he shows, step by step with pictures, how to unclog a kitchen drain with a portable, crank snake. He could link to a product sold on Amazon, giving the ready easy access to exactly the product needed to do the job. How convenient! As an added bonus to the plumber, he could actually have this product linked to an Amazon seller account so that he gets a small commission if/when the reader purchases his recommended product.

Example 3: The plumber could post what the city regulations are for his city in regard to the plumbing codes for new construction. He could link to a .gov site for his local city or county commissioner's office.

Note, it's very simple to locate these .gov, .org or .edu sites. I've included some screenshots below and given you some instructions to follow along.

Full disclosure here, I only use Safari for my web browser. I'm sure Chrome and Firefox have similar advanced search options, but I'm not including those here, because I am not familiar with them.

First, open up a new Google search window, but

instead of typing in the regular search bar, click on "set-tings' in the lower right-hand corner and a menu will pop up.

From there, you want to click on 'advanced settings'. This will take you to an entirely different window that you maybe never even knew existed; one that will give you many different searching capabilities and help you get to answers much more quickly than having to sift through dozens of pages of websites to get to one that would be appropriate for you to use for your business.

There are two fields we are going to pay attention to; in the first field that reads "all these words" type in the word 'plumbing' or 'plumbing tips'.

Important—sometimes adding the words 'tips' or 'hacks' will generate the best results. Try a couple of different phrases if necessary.

In the field several rows down that reads "site or domain", we are going to type in the phrase, '.edu.' What this will do is filter out all the sites other than the .edu sites, giving us a much smaller selection to peruse to select an article to link to for the authority link.

The results will then populate and you will have a plethora of websites to choose from to link to. I can't stress this enough—please read through the articles in their entirety before you link to anything on the internet, even if a friend or colleague recommends it. If you link to it, it's the same as having your name on it. You do not want to have anything that uses profanity in any way, or questionable content. You should not find any of that on a .gov, .edu or .org site, but read through it any way, just to cover your bases.

There are easily 4 articles here that this business could use to link to in their website.

I've given you several examples of ways to create authority links in the copy of your website. These links can be placed in the static content (the information that doesn't change), or in your blogs and articles.

4. YOUR WEBSITE NEEDS AT LEAST THREE POINTS OF CONTACT

Each site should have at least three ways for people to contact your company. Because of how technology has influenced how we communicate, people have different preferences of how they choose to communicate. Some people hate talking on the phone and prefer e-mail, or they hate e-mail and want to talk to someone over the phone or in-person. Having multiple ways for people to contact you makes you and your company more approachable to a broader range of people.

Obviously the first one is a phone number, which should be big and prominent on the home page. If you don't want to put your personal cell out there, get a second line for your business.

If you just want one phone for logistics,

GoDaddy has an incredibly affordable service, around five dollars a month, that will provide you with a business phone number and a greeting, and a recording that will ring through to your own personal number. When you don't want to take calls, or when you are finished for the day, you can set it to 'off office hours' and it will record a message. It can text you that message when it comes in so that you don't miss anything urgent. Or, you can have it emailed to you; there are a number of ways you can manipulate the settings.

A second easy point of contact could be email. Everyone uses email these days and everyone should have an email address on their website that has their domain. If you have your personal email account on your website with a gmail, hotmail, yahoo or dare I say, aol email account on there, get rid of it! It is not doing anything for your credibility. Get a simple email account like info@yourbusiness.com, even if you just have it forwarded to your gmail account. A gmail, or other, email account looks unprofessional on a website. Ditch it.

A contact form on your website is a very easy way for a potential customer to ask you a question. It is standard today for all websites to have a form for people to fill out where they can request more information, or literature, about your products and services. I am not talking about joining a mailing list, though I will address that in a later chapter. Another great option for using an actual contact form is that you can use it as a bit of a vetting process. If you set it up with a few required questions, it will help narrow down truly serious inquiries and will weed out those who are just nosing around.

A mailing address is good to establish creditability in the eyes of the public. It looks 'solid' and credible. The only caveat here is that with Google maps in full play, if your address happens to be in a sketchy part of town, that is what your potential customer is going to see when they use Google Maps to search for your address. An actual picture of your location will show up. Just be mindful of that.

5. DOES YOUR WEBSITE HAVE TARGET KEYWORDS?

Having keywords that your potential clients are searching for is essential to building a web presence. Your Website needs specific targeted keyword phrases to enable the search engines to easily and quickly find you. Done correctly, you will quickly rank in Google and other search engines for these phrases. Remember to verify that your keywords are relevant. If you sell baby diapers, you need to ensure that you are not ranking for adult diapers. Targeted keyword phrases will help you dominate your niche and increase traffic to your website.

A good place to start looking for keywords is the helpful Google Keyword tool. Think of "long-tail keywords", which are easier to rank for. Let me give you an example. When people are ready to buy tires, they don't put 'tires' in the search bar. They put "Best 2012

Mazda 5 tires size xyz", etc. That's a long-tail keyword. Utilize the Google Keyword Tool, but also use common sense and think of how YOU would search.

The simplest way to get started with this is to sit down and make a list of all the services you provide. Those are keywords to get you started. Off of those main words, you can begin to come up with offshoots, additional keywords that would be related to your industry.

My recommendation for using the Google Keyword Tool is to simply do a search and start watching some of the tutorial videos that Google provides. They are very user-friendly and give you step-by-step instructions on how to maneuver through their system. Ubersuggest is another tool I have used for keyword research. At present, you can find that tool here: https:// app.neilpatel.com/en/ubersuggest/ It may be a bit easier to work with than Google's tool for newbies.

You should work these keywords naturally into the copy of your website. Don't 'keyword stuff' your copy so that the verbiage doesn't make sense; you still want the flow to read naturally. Wherever possible, however, you want the Google bots to be able to pick up on the keyword phrases to signal back "Hey, there is significant material over here on this website!" Google always wants to show the most relevant websites to its customers.

6. DOES YOUR WEBSITE HAVE LINKS TO YOUR SOCIAL NETWORKING SITES?

Having links to FaceBook and Twitter, as well as other social media sites, will enable your visitors to "connect" with you. The people in your life including friends, family, and members of clubs and other associations, are able to communicate with you. Additionally, you create another layer of connectedness. Simply put, building and maintaining your web presence also means consistently engaging people and building relationships with them online. Remember: getting to know them offline is also critical. The stronger the relationship, the more likely they will trust you. The fact that they know, like and trust you is essential to your success when you have something to offer. The chances of them buying from you or using your service will greatly increase.

You can simply 'link' to these sites, but a better option is to connect your social media feeds to your site. This way, your viewers can see your latest post or two without leaving your website.

There are many plugins and apps out there now that allow you to put your Facebook feed directly on your website. The same holds true for Twitter and other social media channels. It will be up to you to pick and choose which ones are most appropriate for your business. Obviously, don't choose ones that you are not tending to on a regular basis.

If you don't want the feeds on your website, that's fine. At minimum, have links on your site that will take your viewers directly to your social media pages so people can easily connect with you.

7. DOES YOUR WEBSITE HAVE THE ABILITY TO CAPTURE LEADS?

Your website needs to capture the name and email address of visitors so that you can follow up with them after they have visited your site. Capturing these names helps you build your potential customer database, and it gives you a starting point to connect with those potential customers. Your ability to send emails to them will drive them back to your website. If you are not capturing leads on your website, then you are missing a key opportunity to create life-long customers.

Remember, the more information you request from someone, the less apt they will be to sign up. And, it goes without saying, don't SPAM your viewers. It's fine to use your email and you should, to communicate relevant information, special offers, discounts, etc. But, I think it is super annoying to be emailed sales material every single day after signing up for a freebie. I instantly opt out. Just be mindful as you use your list.

At minimum, you will need an email address. If you can also get a first and last name, that would be wonderful. Having a first name especially, will allow you to communicate to them on a first-name basis and will help build that rapport you are so desperately after.

All of the major email programs like Mailchimp, Constant Contact, IContact, etc., have the ability to build forms which will create an HTML code that can be installed on your site. Once your site is published, this code becomes a 'lead capture', or a box of sorts where the viewer can enter their information. That information then goes to your email program and their name and email address gets added to your list.

If it is set up properly, and if your program is equipped for it, your subscriber will immediately get an automated response with a 'thank you' for subscribing, along with whatever item you are giving away.

And then the magic of automated correspondence can begin. Your sales funnel can begin here!

8. DOES YOUR WEBSITE HAVE AN ACTIVE BLOG?

A blog is a great marketing tool on many levels. It allows you to connect with your current customers. You can also communicate with potential customers. It provides a different type of connection than the website. Blogs are a great way to get current information out on the internet. It also allows you a way to communicate your opinion on various topics that your audience is interested in. Blogs build your personal brand and allow you to really connect with people.

There are endless opportunities to interact with your viewers in your blog. Think of the content you are posting on your social media sites, and just transform that into a blog post. It would be great if you could post once a week, but daily would be incredible! Think of all that unique content you will have spread all over the internet!

If you allow comments on your blog, that is an added way to generate engagement. Be careful though, unless monitored carefully, you can quickly and easily gain a lot of spam. You may want to put your settings on 'needs approval before posting'. This way, the comments get emailed to you for approval before they actually get published. This also helps you to keep tabs on profanity or anything unsavory that you don't want on your site.

Adjacent to a blog page could be a community events page. Those often have a huge draw—especially in small towns. Be careful here to make sure you either use a plug in or app that will drop the events after the calendared date has passed, or go in very often and manually update those events. It will reflect negatively on you if you have an event on your website that occurred 2 weeks ago.

Often, people don't know what to write about in their blog. I have found a great launching point is to start with coming up with the top 20 questions that people ask you about your business. Then, answer those 20 questions in the form of a blog post. You will automatically have 20 blog posts! You will not only be supplying useful, relevant content, but you will be showcasing your expertise and establishing yourself as an authority in your market, which is what you are after.

9. DOES YOUR WEBSITE HAVE VIDEOS ON IT?

Video provides for a more powerful impact, and video is especially important for higher retention rates on your site. These retention rates far exceed text or audio. Sites with videos skyrocket to the top of search engines. With video, it is easier to demonstrate your product or service and people are more likely to buy when they watch and hear your video messages, rather than reading or hearing about it. An added benefit of video is that it can go viral fairly quickly.

You do not need to hire an expensive videographer and you do not need any expensive equipment. In fact, in most cases, you can just use the camera on your phone. Be relaxed and try to sound as natural as possible, with as few 'ums' and verbal pauses as possible. Smile and look welcoming. That's it! Speak into the camera and act as if you were telling a friend about your products and services. Keep an intro video to 30-60 seconds.

A video that goes viral will increase your website's traffic and provide great marketing exposure for your business. Keep in mind that the best websites and blogs incorporate all three ways of communication-audio, video and the written word.

Put your video not only on your website, but also Youtube. And, go ahead and post on all of your social bookmarking sites as well!

If you are not sure where to get started in terms of what to say, think of the 5 "W's" you learned in high school English class. Who, What, When, Where, Why and How.

· Who do you serve?

· What services do you offer?

· What areas do you cover?

· What do you specialize in?

· What sets you apart from your competition?

· When did you start your business?

· Why did you start your business? (a brief history)

You get the idea. Make a list of as many different variables of these questions as you can think of, then use these questions as topics for your blog posts. No one knows your business the way you do. Remember, YOU are the expert in your business.

10. IS YOUR WEBSITE MOBILE-RESPONSIVE?

Today, Google places big emphasis on having a mobile-responsive website. This means your website can be easily viewed on a smart phone, iPad or tablet, as easily as it can be displayed on a laptop or desktop monitor. You MUST have a mobile-optimized website. If your site is more than 5 years old, chances are it may not be mobile-responsive. Note, the words 'mobile-optimized' and 'mobile-responsive' are interchangeable. If you have a Wordpress site, be sure to download a mobile plugin. If you are using a platform like Weebly, Squarespace, Wix, GoDaddy, make sure you are using a current, mobile-responsive template.

This is a non-negotiable. The latest information shows that Google will penalize sites that are not mobile-responsive.

11. IS THERE A TESTIMONIAL ON THE HOME PAGE?

Social Proof is what a testimonial provides. A customer tells others that your business is the place to bring their business. You are a trusted provider of a very important service. There is no better marketing tool than a testimonial, and the very best clearly shows the customer's name and photo.

If your website is set up to allow for 3 or 4 testimonials, all the better. People can sometimes be reluctant to leave a video testimonial, because they are insecure about how they will come across on camera. However, those same people will gladly provide you with a written testimonial. If they have a photo on Facebook, chances are they won't take issue with you asking them to use one of their Facebook photos, along with their first name when you post their written testimonial.

Ideally, getting their review on video is price-less! All they need to do is give a 30-second testimonial with their name and your name and why they enjoyed doing business with you, or why they are so pleased with the outcome of your service. In most cases, all you need to do is ask! Think about your favorite hair dresser, plumber, mechanic, etc. Wouldn't you be happy to leave a written testimonial about their service, *if they asked?* They key is simply to ask.

You can do this a number of ways. Here are a couple of ways to get you started.

- On the bottom of your receipts, have a note printed with a link to your Social Media that reads, "If you received great service today, would you please take a moment and leave me a 5-star review at the link below? If you were not pleased with your service, would you please call me immediately so that I can fix the problem? I very much appreciate your business and I want to make sure every experience you have with our company is a great one!"

- On the bottom of your email signature, have a line that reads, "The greatest compliment you can give me is your positive testimonial. Would you please click on the link below and leave your feedback?"

- Hand out similar verbiage on a business card with a Quick-Response (QR) code that leads to your Social Media or Google Business page where they can leave a positive review/testimonial.

Once the positive review has been posted on your Social Media, you can copy that and post it on your website. Alternatively, you can set up a comment section on your website where clients can leave comments directly.

12. IS A CUSTOM DOMAIN WITH A KEYWORD ATTACHED TO YOUR WEBSITE?

Many people don't really think through their domain name before purchasing it. They also think they can only have one domain, when in fact, they can have many. Not only can you have www.JanzenMarketingLLC.com, but you can also have www.WebsiteDesignSalina.com . It is a good idea to have a keyword in your domain name, if possible. In the case of Website Design Salina, website design is one of the major services we provide. Salina, Kansas is where we are located. I know that people search for "website design salina", so I want my website to come up number one when those keywords are entered.

Not only will my domain name be keyword rich, but I will use those same keywords in my meta descriptions, my photos tags and titles, my permalinks and my page titles. All of this will feed into the overall Search Engine Optimization (SEO) SEO of my website. This is a strategy for filling your website with components that will shout to Google that your website is worthy of being on the first page in search results.

If my business name was something like Angela's Alley, that does not say anything about what my business is all about. Thus, if my domain name was AngelasAlley.com, it may be easy to remember, so okay for a *second* domain, but it really does nothing for SEO. It does nothing to tell my audience, or Google, what my site is about. And if my name was a *totally* random one, it would be even harder to figure out. It seems that in today's business world, companies are trying to come up with clever, cutesy, catchy names that make absolutely no sense whatsoever. I heard an advertisement on talk radio the other day for a company that sells premier sheet sets. I couldn't quite remember the company name, so I guessed at BidoBrand.com , which turned up a site for cannabis for pets. Nope. What I was looking for was bollandbranch.com. I had to wait until I heard it again on the radio and then write it down. Don't make your potential customers have to come look for you.

Some additional things to consider when purchasing your domain:

- Don't overcomplicate it. Try to keep it under 20 characters and easy to spell.

- Do not use underscores or hyphens and try to stay away from numbers. Most people do not remember those things.

- If you found a fantastic domain that is perfect and you are worried about someone copying it, buy up several variations. Buy the .net, .org. .info, etc. versions.

13. IS THERE UNIQUE CONTENT ON EVERY PAGE?

This should go without saying, but make sure that every page on your website has unique content. It's okay to pull some points off your services page and highlight those on your home page, just don't repeat entire pages. Google does not want to see entire websites duplicated for the sake of SEO. In regard to those domains I talked about in the last chapter, please don't be tempted to make one website, copy it twelve times and stick twelve different domains on it. Google will penalize you for that and make take all those sites down indefinitely.

Each page should have a minimum of 2-3 keywords on it. They can be the same keywords if your business is narrow, but if you do many different things, try to highlight 2-3 different keywords on each page.

The same holds true with pictures, infographics,

etc. You will want each page to 'pop' in appearance, so have unique, fresh content throughout your website.

14. IS THERE A CUSTOM TITLE TAG (H1 OR H2) ON EVERY PAGE?

Because content is such a key foundational element for a website's entire SEO plan, we have to address the importance of the headline. You will want to create a strong, descriptive headline for all the content on your site that mentions your keywords. This will help your user understand the topic that your page is about. This will include pages, blog posts, articles, etc.

By using headlines on your pages, there is HTML markup code that is telling your browser that it is a headline. Search engines will look at this headline as a ranking factor for the content of the page. Thus, it is valuable to use keywords in your headlines if possible.

You may recognize these headlines as H1, H2, H3, all the way up to H6 in their labeling. This will be built into the HTML source code of your site and Google will see it. You simply have to select "headline" if you are typing up your content in Word or Pages. You will prepare the body of your document text in 'body' format.

15. DO THE WEBSITE PAGES HAVE TITLE TAGS?

Think of a title tag as SEO for Universal Resource Locators (URLs). It is the location of a page on your website. After you have chosen a domain name, optimizing the title tags, for your pages is the next most important SEO step. The reason for this is because descriptive URLs can help significantly with link building. Search engines will read these URLs to gain insight as to the content of the pages of your website.

As with other usages of your keywords, you don't want to keyword stuff. You want your title tags to help guide your readers to what your website is about. You will have the option to title your pages however you want; don't let them be auto-assigned a name. What makes the most sense for a contact page name? JanzenMarketingLLC.com/Contact-page or JanzenMarketingLLC.com/A22ddf67 ?

16. IS THERE AN INTERNAL LINK STRATEGY IN PLACE?

Links are a very important part of SEO and also make your website much more interesting. External links are links that come from other places back to your website. Internal links are links that are on your site that link to other components on your site.

For instance, just as your menu bar has menu items that link to the various pages of your website, you can have other headers and copy that also link to various places on your site. These links help the search engines crawl (search and remember) your content. Page links can pass page equity (digital-clout) to other pages on your site. This shows the search engines that there is value on other pages of your site—not just your home page.

Your internal links should point to the most relevant and important links on your website. Here is a practical example. On your homepage, you have a copy that highlights the services that you offer at your marketing agency. One of those services is website design. You can build a link from those two words "website design' and have that phrase link to a services page that talks all about your website design services. Or perhaps you have a picture of a recent event on your website of a company fundraiser. You can create an internal link that, when clicked, takes the reader to a blog post that gives a summary of the outcome of that fundraising event.

Internal links will ideally click to places on your site. These are different from links to authority sites that we discussed earlier. Those take people off your site. Internal links take people to other places on your website. You can do this in several ways and several times from the home page.

17. DO ALL IMAGES CONTAIN ALT TAGS AND KEYWORDS?

Images offer another unique SEO opportunities to help you with search engine ranking. Search engines crawl data related to images just like content. They use this data to understand the relevance of a given page. Most of us know how to upload an image, but there are also some effective and simple ways to add additional SEO oomph to your images.

The image alt tag gives search engines context for your image. This tag helps search engines under-stand the meaning of your image so it serves both SEO and accessibility functions. According to the Weebly website building platform, you should "Write an image alt tag for each image you add to your website. A good alt tag can provide extra keyword context for your page and help the image rank higher in image search.

Best practices

- Keep it short, under 125 characters.

- Don't stuff with keywords, keep the text natural and descriptive. Imagine if the image didn't load or someone couldn't see the image what short line of text would accurately describe the context of the image.

- Don't use alt tags on decorative images, like background images."

At minimum, have your images titled properly before uploading them. A photo titled, Website_Design_Janzen_Marketing.png, will be much more attractive to the search engines than a default number-letter, auto-assigned, name of "pgiie7865xg46.png." Simply go in and retitle (rename) the photo before you upload it, using a keyword that is appropriate to the page. Every picture on your website should be properly titled with an SEO/keyword rich title and not just a generic one.

18. DOES EACH IMAGE HAVE A PROPER URL AND FILENAME?

As I stated in the previous chapter, adding keywords to your image filenames is another technique designed to provide even more weight to your SEO strategy. Search engines will look at filenames in images for context on an image. This gives you another opportunity to rank in image search and helps with your website's overall ranking for that specific keyword. An optimized image URL helps your image appear in image search and makes it easier to link and share your image. Be sure to create short, concise names for each image that convey your most important keywords.

Keep in mind that image size can have an effect how fast your website will load. It's important to have pages that load quickly. Google deems it important that website load quickly, and you don't want your viewers to be waiting on your images to load.

There are free tools out there to resize your images. Two of my favorites are Canva and Fotor.

19. ARE THERE META DESCRIPTIONS ON EVERY PAGE?

A meta description is a piece of copy that summarizes the content belonging to a page of your website. It is displayed on the search engine results page (SERP) below the headline.

Keywords in the meta description are very important for clickthrough and engagement. Potential users will read your meta description while searching and will make a decision about whether or not to visit your site, making this an extremely valuable SEO element to driving traffic from the search results page to your site.

Be sure to write a description that is engaging and interesting, and one that includes relevant keywords and important terms. It's okay to include brand names and a call-to-action. Remember, if someone is searching for one of your keywords, and sees it explained in your meta description, they are highly likely to click on your link over another website.

Keep your meta description characters between 150-160 as that is how many Google shows in the Search Engine Results Page (SERP).

If possible, use power-words like "free" and "now" and "learn". They've been proven to be highly 'clickable'.

20. HAS THE GOOGLE BUSINESS PAGE BEEN VERIFIED AND OPTIMIZED?

Google Places for Business, Google Listings, and Google+ Business Pages are now being covered under one product, Google Business Profile. You MUST do this step if you want your business to show up in a Google search. It is the single most important thing you need to do.

Google My Business is a free tool that allows you to promote your Business Profile and business website on Google Search and Maps. With your Google My Business account, you can see and connect with your customers, post updates to your Business Profile, and see how customers are interacting with your business on Google.

It's simple to do, but it does take a few minutes and as the business owner, you need to be the one to do it. If you have an agency verify and optimize your page, that's fine. But you will need to be on the other end of a text for 3 minutes while the codes get texted back and forth. That's one of Google's verification methods to make sure it is indeed the business owner who is claiming that business's page.

To claim, verify and optimize your Google Business profile, simply google "Google My Business" and it will lead you through a series of prompts. Once you have verified your page, you may begin uploading video, pictures, details, etc. about your business. You will find this step to be of great value and many people know nothing about it.

21. IS THERE AN SSL CERTIFICATE ATTACHED TO THE SITE?

First of all, what is an SSL certificate? SSL stands for Secure Socket Layer. It used to be that just Ecommerce or membership sites needed an SSL certificate. Now, however, Google is making it an unspoken requirement to have one unless you want the 'name of shame' mark in the web address bar next to your domain name.

First, let me give you the technical explanation, according to GoDaddy, of what and SSL certificate is and does. They can explain the details far better than I can.

"An SSL (Secure Sockets Layer) certificate is a digital certificate that authenticates the identity of a website and encrypts information sent to the server using SSL technology. Encryption is the process of scrambling data into an undecipherable format that can only be returned to a readable format with the proper decryption key.

A certificate serves as an electronic "passport" that establishes an online entity's credentials when doing business on the Web. When an Internet user attempts to send confidential information to a Web server, the user's browser accesses the server's digital certificate and establishes a secure connection.

An SSL certificate contains the following information:

- The certificate holder's name
- The certificate's serial number and expiration date
- A copy of the certificate holder's public key
- The digital signature of the certificate-issuing authority"

Now, if you have an SSL certificate, your website name will appear with a lock next to the name. If you don't have an SSL certificate, you will have the words "not secure" printed next to your website name. Start looking around the internet and you will see what I am talking about. I don't like to call people out, but this truly hurts public persona when the words "not secure" show up next to a business name. Your site may be perfectly safe, 100% clean with no malware, etc., but if you don't have an SSL certificate, it will show up that way.   Also, Google now brings this into great consideration when choosing how to rank websites. Please keep this in mind as you are optimizing your website. Buy an SSL certificate and put it in place.

22. ARE GOOGLE WEBMASTER TOOLS BEING UTILIZED?

Google Search Console (known as Webmaster Tools) is one of the most important single tools to use for SEO. You need to do this step to submit your website to the Google index. Please don't be intimidated by this step as it is not difficult. Just go slowly and follow the steps I have outlined.

By this time, you will have already verified your Google business listing. You must use your Gmail account to sign into webmaster tools.

Step 1: Once signed into your Gmail account, click on the right upper-hand 'square' with the 9 dots inside.

Step 2: From there, scroll down and click on the 'webmaster tools' icon. That will lead you to a screen like this one.

Step 3: From here, follow the 'start now' prompts. This will take you to the area where you need to verify that you do indeed own the site and the domain. You will have a variety of ways you can verify the domain. Follow the instructions until you have the domain verified.

From here, you will want to follow through with the beginner's steps. Make sure you complete all the steps to 'index' your site and submit a sitemap. You will want to resubmit a sitemap every time you make major changes or updates to your website. Google will send you follow up email with some very helpful tools and steps you can follow. I suggest you do follow these steps to make sure you are utilizing all their free tools completely.

"This is your best connection directly to Google and understanding how your website is crawled, indexed and generally interpreted by Google. You can use the Search Console to get alerts when there are problems, and to provide Google with important information about changes and updates to your content. It also serves as an incredibly valuable keyword tracking tool. (and it's free!)".

23. HAS A SITEMAP BEEN SUBMITTED TO GOOGLE?

A sitemap is like a blueprint for your website. If you think of your website like a house, and the pages like rooms in your house, a sitemap would be the blueprint which shows people (Google and other search engines) how to navigate through your site to get to the information they need. Sitemaps help Google a find and index your content quickly. Some website platforms automatically generate a sitemap for you.

To access your sitemap simply add / sitemap.xml to the end of your homepage. For example the sitemap for JanzenMarketingLLC.com is available at https://www.JanzenMarketingLLC.com/sitemap.xml

You can submit your sitemap directly to Google through Google Search Console to make sure Google finds and crawls all your pages.

1.	Visit https://www.google.com/webmasters/ tools

2.	Sign up and verify your site - or just log in if you already have your site verified

3.	Go the Crawl > Sitemaps from the left-hand navigation

4.	Click Add/Test Sitemap

5.	Add sitemap.xml into the text box

6.	Click Submit

If you're adding a lot of content to your site on a daily basis, resubmit your sitemap weekly. If you're not making a lot of changes, just resubmit anytime you do something major.

Here's a tip: you can type in 'site:www.yourwebsitedomain.com ' into a search bar to find your indexed pages.

24. ARE THERE SOCIAL MEDIA CONNECTIONS IN PLACE?

Sites such as Facebook allow you to create a Fan Page to assist in creating community, sharing information and building trust. Using social media is a free and easy way to market your website, and also connect directly with your current and potential clients. More and more people are using social networking sites as resources to find information on products and services. Social media is here to stay. It is truly important you find a way to use it, and evolve with it, in order to build your web presence.

Drill down deeper here and utilize Facebook groups and events in addition to just having a business page.

LinkedIn now has a set-up where you can have a business page as well as start a group. What a great way to show your authority! Start a LinkedIn group in your niche and begin inviting people. We will discuss LinkedIn in another chapter.

Here are some ways to use Social Media to help you with your website. Remember that your goal is to not only create links back to your website, but to create relationships that will help you in the future. By doing these activities, you are using SEO strategies that will help your website grow your business.

1. **Find like-minded people in your industry.** Find bloggers, writers, other small business owners who are willing to talk and/or collaborate with you. Start with people in your local area. Find them and invite them out for coffee and start strategizing! Figure out some ways that you could possibly partner on some projects. There truly is enough business out there for everyone. There may be something that you do in your business that they don't do, or vice-versa, and you can refer business back and forth.

2. **Leverage your current relationships.** You can reach out to your friends, customers, vendors, anyone that you are currently doing business with to see if you can swap links. Perhaps you can find a way to put their link on our website, and they will put yours

on theirs. Be sure you know their site well and that it will be appropriate for your audience.

3. **Be mindful of your market**. Follow what is going on with the players in your market. A simple way to do this is through Google alerts. We will discuss setting up Google Alerts in another chapter. This is a great way to be notified when someone posts about your business, or a topic pertaining to your business. Then, reach out to them and start a conversation. Hopefully, a collaboration will result.

4. **Use hashtags** Tag a business, or an influencer and you are highly likely to get a response from them. People are very likely to respond to you since this is a public forum. Keep your note short, sweet and complimentary for the best feedback. Again, your goal is to get your foot in the door to find a good target, and then begin building relationships from there.

5. **Get local and network** Get active in your community's local Business Network International (BNI) group or Chamber of Commerce. These places offer member lists on their websites and will link back to your website. They generally prove to be helpful authority links and can provide great traction for your site. Don't be afraid to get out there and network. Meet some people and

discuss how you can work together to help each other with your website traffic.

25. HAS DUPLICATE CONTENT BEEN ELIMINATED?

This one is a no-brainer. Go through your site and make sure that accidental duplicate content has been eliminated. I'm not talking about content that you deliberately want to put on the home page as well as on the services page, but rather pages that you may have inadvertently copied and posted by accident. It happens.

Just give your site a thorough once-over, or have your proofreader do this, to make sure you do not have huge passages of copy that has been duplicated on multiple pages, or that you've used the same image on four different pages, etc.

As mentioned in an early chapter, Google wants unique, relevant content on every page of your website.

26. HAVE ALL DEAD PAGES BEEN CLEANED UP?

This is one that is easy to miss. It seems like it would be easy enough to catch, but if your site is several years old and many layers deep, it is very possible that you have some dead pages. By dead pages, I mean pages that turn up an error when you visit them. You need to either delete them, or fix them. Do not leave them on your website with the thought that you will come back and fix them later, because you may very well forget.

It looks unprofessional to have dead pages on your site. We've all done it. We have a page from a few years ago that perhaps led to a product, or a blog that is no longer in existence (and we may not even know it). Check your site monthly for dead pages and get rid of them.

27. HAS THE SITE BEEN SUBMITTED TO THE TOP 50 ONLINE DIRECTORIES?

Think of online directories as the old-fashioned Yellow Pages of yesterday. Only now, there are thousands of these and they are online sites. There are paid sites, but many of them are free. You do not need to be on all of them, but you should be on the top 50 most related to your business. And, you most definitely want to be on the most popular search engines overall.

First off, make sure you are listed on Google Business. Then you will want to be listed on:
- Yahoo Business
- Bing Local
- Yelp
- Trip Advisor (if relevant)
- YP

After this, do a Google search for "top 50 online directories for <insert your business category> and see what the results are. I did a local search for "top 40 online directories for Chiropractors". Once you have that list, begin applying to those locations or listings with your business information. It's a bit time-consuming, but it will pay off. Keep a spreadsheet to stay organized.

Alternatively, you can hire companies like Bright Local to do this work for you. You simply contact them, tell them what you want, pay them a monthly fee, and they will take care of submitting and managing the listings for you.

Either method will help tremendously in getting your website to move towards page one of a Google search.

28. HAVE GOOGLE ANALYTICS BEEN INSTALLED AND UTILIZED?

Setting up Google Analytics on your site is extremely important. First of all, this will not only tell you how many people are looking at your site, but how long they are staying on each page. Remember I said that Google is all about engagement. If people are only on your site for 1 second, you need to figure out why. If there are errors on your site, Google Analytics will tell you so, and then you can fix those errors. It may not be that your content is bad, it may be that you have technical errors that need fixing.

To set up Google Analytics, open your Chrome browser.

1.   Before exiting, click on the 'user' tab, which is directly to the right of the 'admin' tab at the top of the page, scroll down to the lower right-hand side of the page and click 'save'.

2.   That's it! You're all set up. Reading analytics and making fixes will be in another book.

BONUS SECTION

29. IS EMAIL MARKETING IN PLACE THAT DRIVES TRAFFIC BACK TO THE SITE?

Emailing existing and prior customers is a great way to stay in touch with them. There is no better way to remind them of the services you offer. Using email is also a very cost-effective and a good way to increase sales. Another great advantage of using email marketing is that you can directly measure your return on investment. Use email to ask for and receive feedback from your customers about your product and services. (The responses and requests may surprise you!)

30. IS THERE A SPECIAL REPORT OR CHECKLIST TO GIVE AWAY?

A special report or checklist delivered to the captured email address is a great way to begin a relationship and stay connected to current and potential customers. People enjoy receiving useful information that applies to them, especially if it improves their lives. By becoming a reliable source of information, you are building trust and establishing a relationship that will lead more people to buy from you or use your service. If you are not currently providing this type of information, begin by simply asking your customers what they would like to receive from you.

A great idea starter would be to make a list of the top 10 questions you get asked in your business, then answer those. You can put your answers in the form of a checklist, infographic, special report, podcast, etc. and then give it away!

This need not be something new that you have to create. Go back through newsletters you have written or informational reports you have drafted. If you have been in business more than a year, you will have this data already put together in form or another.

There is your special report! Have a graphic designer create an attractive cover for it and you will have a nice pdf that you can hand out to people in exchange for their contact information.

You are the expert in your business. People ask you questions every day. Just think about those most frequently asked questions, write them down, and answer them. It will come together easier than you think. A special report does not need to be 12 pages long; it may only be 2 pages long. That's okay. The point is that you are giving them something of value. You want to give them information that they did not know prior to coming to your site.

Checklists are also great for give-aways in exchange for an email address. Something like an "Home

Winterizing Checklist" would be a great give-a-way for a plumber or HVAC company. The end goal is to establish yourself as the authority in your market. Always keep that in mind, no matter what kind of materials you are developing.

31. ARE RELATIONSHIP NURTURING AUTORESPONDERS ENABLED?

You may wonder how this is different from capturing their name. Well, autoresponders automatically send out a 'personalized' e-mail message on a specific day, time, or in response to a query from a client or prospect. Capturing their name and e-mail is not enough. You must do something with it. Autoresponders are a great way to constantly keep in contact and connect with your current and potential clients and customers. A simple 'thank you for joining', followed by useful information is a great way to create new and lifelong customers. A big tip is to just be yourself in these emails. It is essential to remember the goal is to connect with people, and the best way to do that is by showing them who you are, and why they should trust you.

My earlier remarks about establishing a lead capture also apply here. Beyond this, you need to establish a 'drip campaign'. This is where your email campaign sends out periodic materials automatically to your subscribers. These materials need to be relevant and helpful, not spammy junk. They can certainly be coupons and special offers. This goes a step beyond the scope of what is needed on a website, but I feel it is a necessary step in keeping that client once you have their name collected from your website.

32. ARE REVIEWS BEING POSTED TO GOOGLE BUSINESS PAGE?

Google is on fire about reviews right now! Do everything within your power as a business owner to get your customers to post good reviews on your Google business page. There is nothing Google loves to see more, and will respect more, than REAL positive reviews.

Never, ever fabricate positive reviews and don't hire any agency that does. Not only is it unethical, but Google will shut your website down in a heartbeat if they suspect you are doing this. I'll list a few ways below, but you can get creative also.

- Ask! 'Ms. Customer, if we delivered top-notch service to you today, would you please take a moment to leave us a positive review on our Google Business page?
- Email! On the bottom of every email, include a link to your Google Business page and repeat a phrase like the one above.

· Put it on your invoices! On the bottom of your invoices, include a link to your Google Business page and repeat the phase like the one above.

33. ARE THERE RELEVANT ARTICLES SHOWCASING YOUR EXPERTISE?

Posting on your blog and writing short, concise relevant information in an article are very different. The articles you write should show off the depth of your knowledge. It helps prove your skill and expertise, and it reinforces your authority. Articles need to stand the test of time and are often referred to as evergreen. Articles can be used as reference points for blogs posts and submitted to various article directories such as Ezines.com to establish yourself with a wider audience.

A blogpost can be about 150 words, with or without a picture attached. An article will be more like 750 words. Go in depth here.

34. IS THERE AN ACTIVE PAY PER CLICK CAMPAIGN?

Google Ads are another way to drive more business to your website. You can rank fairly quickly. How long you rank for that day depends on your budget. Here is how it works.

Let's say my Google ads budget is $10 per day. I have 50 various keywords I am ranking for, all related to the marketing field. Let's say that, on average, my keywords are costing me $2 per click. That means that my ads will show until they have been clicked on 5 times that day. ($2 x 5 = $10 budget). If those clicks happen in 5 hours, that means my ad was shown for 5 hours. If those clicks happened in 5 minutes, that means my ad was shown for 5 minutes. You can quickly burn through your Google Ads budget.

My personal experience is that if you don't have $300 per month to put towards Google Adwords, don't bother. Google won't give you an Adwords Account Manager if you can't commit to that level either.

Now, having said that, my clients that I currently have on Google Ads are doing extremely well with them. They are in the number 1 position and the phone is consistently ringing off the hook—which is what we want. Make sure you are working with an agency who will meet with you every month to review your stats and explain where your money is going and show you your Ads dashboard. You don't want to be paying an agency $500 per month for Google Ads only to find out they are only spending $100 on Google Ads. Follow up.

35. IS THE BLOG CONNECTED TO SOCIAL BOOKMARKING SITES?

Digg and De.li.cious are two examples of social bookmarking sites. Users can "vote" on the content of your site. These votes increase the number of visits by others since they were directed by these "votes".

The bookmarks themselves become a source of traffic to your site, and they offer an additional channel for the promotion of your content. Many search engines use the categorization and description of each bookmark to understand the content of the webpage. The bookmark effectively becomes another way to show that your site is relevant, and relevancy will always increase traffic to your website.

What you will need to do is to go to these websites and open an account. I would recommend you get a spreadsheet and write down the name of the site on the left, your username and password, etc., for easy re-trieval in case you lose your login credentials. Some sites you can automatically connect your blog to dir-ectly from your website platform. Others, you will have to upload manually. If you sit down and do this in one afternoon, it won't take long.

Remember this important task. At the bottom of every blog that you put on your website (and then onto theses social bookmarking sites), you need to in-clude your company information. And, include a back-link to your website! I'll give you an example below:

Janzen Marketing, LLC

https://JanzenMarketingLLC.com

info@JanzenMarketingllc.com

785-201-3331

As of the time of this writing, these are the basic sites you want to be on:

blogster

twitter

wordpress

xing

stumpleupon

storify

tagged

skyrock

app.net

bibsonomy

bitly

delicious

diigo

feedspot

folkd

friendfeed

hi5

instapaper

jumptags

kaboodle

kippt

linkagogo

livejournal

referral key

pocket

newswine

myaol

36. ARE THERE SOCIAL SHARING CAPABILITIES ON ALL ARTICLES, BLOGS, CONTENT?

Using Instagram to connect is another way to engage your website to followers interested in your specific product or service. Instagram is one of the fastest growing social media platforms and already has millions of active users. Many companies are already using Instagram as a marketing tool to drive traffic to their websites. You do not want to miss this opportunity to connect with people. People use Instagram to find a steady stream of ideas, links, resources, content and valuable tips. If you are the one who is providing them, then people are going to be buying from you.

The same holds true with Pinterest and LinkedIn. We know Facebook is an old standby and so is Twitter. Don't be afraid to try a new social media platform to expand your business and potential reach a new audience. Share, share, share!

37. IS THERE A LINKEDIN COMPANY PAGE?

LinkedIn is a great way to connect with a variety of business professionals. Along with Facebook and Twitter, LinkedIn is considered to be one of the top social networking sites. It is a great way to network and also get the name of your business out there to other professionals. LinkedIn can also be used as a resource to do research on current and potential clients. LinkedIn should not be overlooked when promoting yourself and your business.

Most people have heard of LinkedIn and may even have a personal profile. But, are you aware that there are LinkedIn Company pages? It's there! You can fill out your company page just the same as you would fill out a Facebook Business Page. I'll show you how.

First, click on the 'work' button on top, next to your profile picture, and then scroll down to 'create a company page'. There you can follow the prompts to set up your company page.

When you want to toggle back and forth from your personal profile to your business profile, simply click on the drop-down arrow next to your picture and scroll to the bottom.

What you can end up with is a fantastic looking platform that you can post to, just like your Facebook business page. But you don't have to sift through all the pictures of kittens and puppies to get down to business. You can get right to the customers you want to reach. You can also have access to LinkedIn ads, just like Facebook ads.

38. IS THERE AN RSS FEED?

Real Simple Syndication is also known as an RSS feed. It is an easy way to distribute your information across the internet. It allows you to create a channel with your content so that it automatically sends your info out each time you post something new on your website. The more readers, subscribers and websites that opt to your RSS feed, the more targeted traffic you will receive to your website. RSS helps you connect with people in real time and increase your rankings in the various search engines.

You can share news about your RSS feed through your Social Media accounts, your email, by word of mouth, through direct mail, through your networking groups, etc. The main idea is to get the word out there that people can now easily follow all the great stuff that is happening at your business simply by subscribing to your RSS feed.

If you are uncertain as to how to do this, again, watch some YouTube videos or stay tuned for my upcoming Beta course where I will be doing a video tutorial walk-through on every step in this book.

39. IS THERE A REPUTATION MARKETING STRATEGY IN PLACE?

Reputation *Management* allows you to keep close tabs on what is being said about you online. It allows you to track down those good reviews and give them a thank you by email, phone call, etc. It also allows you to read the bad reviews and give them an immediate action. You especially want to follow up on poor reviews within the first 24 hours.

Reputation Marketing goes one step further. It does the above monitoring and management steps, but it solicits reviews from your customers. This can be done in a number of different ways.

1. Have a review site on your website. You will want to have all comments come to you, the business owner. This site may or may not be a public page. What you can do is to take that information and act on it. Give each reviewer a call, or an email. What a great, per-

sonal touch that will go a long way in relationship building.

2. Hand out a biz card with 2 QR codes that lead to 2 different places. A green QR code with a smiley face leads to a page on your website where they can leave a positive review. The red QR code with a mad face leads to an email address that goes directly to the owner for immediate handling.

3. Although you shouldn't pay (directly) for reviews, there's nothing wrong with asking your customers to go onto your FB, Google Business, or Yelp account and leaving a positive review. If it is your policy to give out more *practical* thank-yous to those people who take the time to leave a review, that may be appreciated, too.

40. IS THERE A LINK TO A PODCAST ON THE WEBSITE?

Podcasts are not only easy to do, once you get started, but they are really *fun*. Most people don't know that you can create, edit and publish a podcast for FREE. There are tools out there that will walk you through the whole creation process. You do not need to have any fancy equipment, just a decent microphone will do. I know some business owners that use their smart phone to record their podcasts. Once recorded, you load them to a podcast site and publish. It really is that easy.

Imagine having the clout and prestige of having a link to your own podcast on your website! How cool is that? With a simple graphic software creator, like Canva (free), you can create your podcast cover and up-load your design to your podcast 'launchpad'. There are many YouTube videos out there on how to get started creating your own podcast.

At the time of this writing, I am putting together a video course which will walk my readers through every step of this book in video format. I will include step-by-step instructions for creating a podcast, if that is something that interests you. You will truly be thought of as the expert in your field if you have your own podcast on your website!

41. IS THERE PERSONAL BRANDING OF THE BUSINESS OWNER?

If an individual is being branded as the recognizable figure or "face" of your business, you want to make sure that his or her name is on the first page of Google. More importantly, you want to make sure all references are positive. Any negative references or stories may hurt the business' reputation and ultimately cost you sales. If you do not know how your business is being perceived, now is the time to find out so that you can create steps to change or maintain it.

Open an incognito window to do the search for the business owner and see what comes up. If it's favorable, great! If it's not, start taking some steps to suppress or fix the problem.

42. ARE THERE NEW AND RELEVANT PLUGINS?

Plugins allow you to add features and functions to your website without having to learn coding or programming. Some of the new and relevant plugins help you keep visitors on your site, without them using a link and leaving your site. There are plug-ins that are designed to help you with search engine optimization (SEO), and plugins that get more targeted traffic to your website. Keeping up to date on the latest plugins and how they can be integrated into your website will help you improve your web presence.

There are now plugins for everything you can imagine. Pop-up plugins can be installed on your site that act as a lead capture to collect a name and address for people. They will be activated by a certain trigger, like when someone is about to leave your site, or when they have been on your site for x number of seconds.

There are plugins that allow for your Facebook, Twitter, Instagram feeds to be shown on your website automatically. Some have built-in SEO components. Some can help with mailing lists. There are literally hundreds of different functionalities available now in regard to plugins and website apps. Start reading up and checking out ones that you think would be important to you and your viewers.

43. ARE COMMENTS ENABLED TO ENCOURAGE ENGAGEMENT?

Comments allow visitors to your site to engage with and contribute to your site. Allowing comments gives you another chance to connect with your visitors and draws them back to your site. By allowing your site to be more interactive, you differentiate yourself from your competitors, and it signals to your customers and potential customers that you care about their opinions. Just make sure to set up to allow 'comments-with approval first' on your site so that you can monitor what is placed on the site. This precaution is not intended to censor the valuable negative feedback provided; rather, it is to ensure that hateful idiots are not allowed to ruin your efforts.

I also like to add that additional layer of protection by utilizing Captcha. I don't have time to read through all the automated spam that can come through. I use the premium version of the Wordpress plugin, Clean Talk.

While engagement can be a wonderful thing, it can also become a monster in and of itself. If you begin getting hundreds of comments a day, you may need to hire someone to monitor this traffic. It really does depend on the nature of your website and the purpose of your site. If you are trying to reach, connect and establish relationships with people through your site, comments will be a necessity. If you are selling plumbing fixtures, comments may be better handled by a customer service phone line.

Alternatively, you may consider setting up a private Facebook group where your 'tribe' can post, engage, interact and ask questions. You could also host Facebook live videos there where you engage with your audience, answer Q and A, etc. You can always then take that video content and transform it into a blog post for your website. The possibilities are endless!

44. ARE PRESS RELEASES DONE QUARTERLY?

Press releases allow prospects and clients to hear about accomplishments and any awards or other relevant information occurring with you, your website and your company. Press releases allow you to share your story and build a reputation in the community. Posting press releases provides visitors information and stories about you. These stories need to intrigue, interest and entertain people in order to keep them coming back to your website for more. The added bonus of creating press releases is that the media might even pick up your story, and you will receive some free publicity.

Some sources for distributing your press releases are:

prweb.com
newswire.com
ereleases.com

prnewswire.com

If you can get approved to post on Apple News, that's the ultimate place to be. We post all of our clients' press releases there, in front of millions.

45. IS A NEWSLETTER OR MINI-COURSE OFFERED TO ESTABLISH AUTHORITY?

An online magazine or Ezine, mini-course or newsletter delivered to the captured email address is a great way to begin a relationship and stay connected to your current and potential clients. People enjoy receiving useful information that applies to them, especially if it improves their lives. By becoming a reliable source of information, you are building trust and establishing a relationship that will lead more people to buy from you or use your service. If you are not currently providing this type of information, begin by simply asking your customers what they would like to receive from you.

It is easy in today's technical market to offer a course to your viewers or customers. Simply create the videos, set up a membership site, decide what you will charge and you can be up and running in a couple of weeks. This is the ultimate in establishing authority.

If you don't already have an email list, you can still create a newsletter or Ezine and post it on your website. You can have people subscribe to view it, or just have it available directly from your site. Setting up a link from your Facebook page is easy. That will connect to your website and will allow them to transition from your social media to your site with just a click.

We will be launching a Beta course with step by step video instructions of each of these steps. If you would like advance notice of this course, you may sign up at JanzenMarketingLLC.com/coursenotice and we will notify you when the course becomes available for enrollment.

Angela Fairbanks